ABRAHAM LINCOLN

AND THE GETTYSBURG ADDRESS:

SEPARATING FACT FROM FICTION

by Nel Yomtov

CAPSTONE PRESS
a capstone imprint

Capstone Captivate is published by Capstone Press, an imprint of Capstone.
1710 Roe Crest Drive
North Mankato, Minnesota 56003
www.capstonepub.com

Library of Congress Cataloging-in-Publication Data
Names: Yomtov, Nelson, author.
Title: Abraham Lincoln and the Gettysburg Address : separating fact from
fiction / by Nel Yomtov.
Description: North Mankato, Minnesota : Capstone, 2021. | Series: Fact vs. fiction in U.S. history |
Includes bibliographical references and index. | Audience: Ages 8–11 | Audience: Grades 4–6 | Summary:
"In 1863, Abraham Lincoln gave a speech in Gettysburg, Pennsylvania. Since then, the famous speech has led to many stories about it-but not all of them are true. Discover what's real and what's fiction through expertly leveled text containing primary sources"— Provided by publisher.
Identifiers: LCCN 2020044586 (print) | LCCN 2020044587 (ebook) | ISBN 9781496695642 (hardcover) | ISBN 9781496696748 (paperback) | ISBN 9781977153784 (pdf) | ISBN 9781977155528 (kindle edition)
Subjects: LCSH: Lincoln, Abraham, 1809-1865. Gettysburg address—Juvenile literature. | United States—History—Civil War, 1861-1865—Juvenile literature.
Classification: LCC E475.55 .Y66 2021 (print) | LCC E475.55 (ebook) | DDC
973.7/349—dc23
LC record available at https://lccn.loc.gov/2020044586
LC ebook record available at https://lccn.loc.gov/202004458

Image Credits
Library of Congress: 6, 7, 8, 10, 15, 16, 21, 23, Abraham Lincoln Papers, 9; The New York Public Library: 18; Shutterstock: Andriy Blokhin, cover (top left), 28, Bob Pool, 27, Everett Historical, cover (bottom right), back cover, 5, Jon Bilous, 26, Morphart Creation, cover (bottom left), Rosemarie Mosteller, 24, Uncle Leo, cover (top right); USDA: 13; Wikimedia: 17

Editorial Credits
Editor: Gena Chester; Designer: Kyle Grenz; Media Researcher: Svetlana Zhurkin; Production Specialist: Katy LaVigne

Source Notes
p. 8, "be present, and participate . . ." Wills, David, An Official Invitation to Gettysburg, November 2, 1863, loc.gov/exhibits/treasures/tr00.html#obj27
p. 16, "written in the . . ." Allen Thorndike Rice. *Reminiscences of Abraham Lincoln, by Distinguished Men of his Time.* New York: North American Review, 1888, p. 228.
p. 22, "the crowd was hushed . . ." Gettysburg Speech Site, Nd. abrahamlincolnonline.org/lincoln/tours/gettycem2.htm#:~:text=The%20crowd%20was%20hushed%20into,as%20they%20said%20it%20was!%22
p. 22, "Hats were removed . . ." *The Pennsylvania Magazine of History and Biography.* Philadelphia: Historical Society of Pennsylvania, 1909, p. 393.
p. 22, "scarcely could an untearful . . ." Michael Burlingame. *Abraham Lincoln: A Life.* Baltimore: The Johns Hopkins University Press, 2008, p. 222.
p. 22, "His little speech . . ." *New York Times*, November 20, 1863, rmc.library.cornell.edu/gettysburg/ideas_more/reactions_p1.htm
p. 22, "will live among . . ." Ibid.
p. 22, " a monumental act . . ." Cornell University, Nd. rmc.library.cornell.edu/gettysburg/ideas_more/reactions_p3.htm#:~:text=Charles%20Sumner%3A%20%22That%20speech%2C,%20He%20was%20mistaken
p. 24, "silly remarks . . ." CBS News, November 15, 2013, cbsnews.com/news/150-years-later-pa-newspaper-apologizes-for-panning-gettysburg-address/
p. 25, "I should be glad . . ." NPS.gov, Nd. nps.gov/gett/planyourvisit/national-cemetery-virtual-tour.htm

All internet sites appearing in back matter were available and accurate when this book was sent to press.

Printed in the United States   4615

Table of Contents

Words in **bold** are in the glossary.

Introduction

Many people know of President Lincoln's Gettysburg Address. It's one of the most famous speeches in American history. But people might not know the details, the facts, and the fiction surrounding this moment of history.

Lincoln spoke at the **dedication** of the Gettysburg National Cemetery to honor the soldiers who had died in the July 1863 Civil War battle. His speech was only 272 words long and lasted about two minutes. Yet the short speech held a strong message. "These dead shall not have died in **vain**," Lincoln said. Instead, their lives inspired the country to create "a new birth of freedom" where democracy would "not perish from the earth."

Abraham Lincoln delivers his Gettysburg Address.

Fact!

More than 50,000 Union and Confederate soldiers were killed or injured in the Battle of Gettysburg.

Chapter One

The Road to Gettysburg

In the years that followed, many myths arose surrounding Lincoln's Gettysburg Address. Some myths touch on how and where the speech was written. Others involve Lincoln's role at the dedication and the public's reaction to the speech.

Abraham Lincoln in 1864

One of the most common myths is that Lincoln was the main speaker that day. In truth, Edward Everett was the featured speaker. Everett was America's best speaker at the time. He had served in both houses of Congress and as U.S. Secretary of State. On September 23, 1863, Everett received an invitation to speak. He was asked to give the speech on October 23. He said the earliest he could be ready was November 19. The event organizers agreed to move it to that date.

Edward Everett

An Invitation to Speak

President Lincoln did not receive a letter of invitation to speak until November 2. It came from David Wills, a Gettysburg lawyer. Wills was one of the organizers of the dedication. He asked Lincoln to "be present, and participate in these Ceremonies." He also suggested Lincoln deliver only "a few appropriate remarks."

Gettysburg, Pennsylvania, in 1863

Letter to Lincoln inviting him to attend the dedication at Gettysburg

Lincoln did not immediately accept the invitation. He thought his duties at the White House might keep him from going to Gettysburg. Then, on November 16, Lincoln decided to go.

Why Did Lincoln Go?

Lincoln believed the trip to Gettysburg would give him the opportunity to pay his respects to the soldiers who died in the fighting. In the battle, Union troops of the North beat back an invasion by Confederate forces. Lincoln also believed it was important for people from the U.S. government to go to the dedication. Lincoln was going in order to attend a **solemn** event, not to make a major speech.

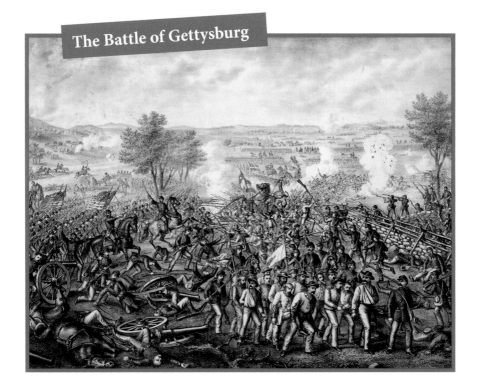

The Battle of Gettysburg

Everett Speaks

Edward Everett spoke for two hours. He blamed the Confederacy for starting a war against the United States. He praised the Union victory at Gettysburg. The crowd applauded Everett's speech. Yet Lincoln's much shorter speech is better remembered because he spoke about equality and freedom for all Americans. His message was timeless. It was something Americans could find meaning in after the Civil War. Because of this, Lincoln's speech—not Everett's—has endured to this day. That is why many people think he was the main speaker at Gettysburg.

Fact!

Everett's speech was emotional and moving. The *Boston Journal* reported, "Scarcely a dry eye was visible, the President mingling his tears with those of the people."

Chapter Two

A Sudden Stroke of Inspiration?

Another myth claims that Lincoln wrote his speech in a burst of **inspiration** while riding the train to Gettysburg. This is not true. Lincoln gave serious thought to his "few appropriate remarks" from the time he accepted the invitation to speak.

On November 17, the evening before he left, Lincoln met with William Saunders at the White House. Saunders had designed the cemetery. He showed Lincoln drawings of the cemetery's layout. Lincoln asked Saunders questions to better understand the battle and the sacrifices made by the soldiers.

After the meeting, Lincoln sat down and began writing his speech. It opened with the now-famous words, "Four score and seven years ago. . . ."

William Saunders worked for the U.S. Department of Agriculture as a botanist and landscape designer.

Fact!

A score is a unit of measure that means 20. So when Lincoln said "Four score and seven years ago," he meant 87 years ago.

The Train Ride to Gettysburg

Lincoln's train left Washington, D.C., at noon on November 18. Members of his **cabinet** and other **politicians** rode with him. The six-hour train ride to Gettysburg, Pennsylvania, was bumpy. The cars rocked as they moved along the tracks. These were not the best conditions for writing a speech by hand.

Lincoln chatted with other people on the train. At each station the train stopped. Lincoln greeted those who turned out to see him. No firsthand accounts at the time mentioned anything about Lincoln writing on the train. Lincoln's secretary, John Nicolay, and his assistant secretary, John Hay, were on the train with Lincoln. Both men denied Lincoln wrote anything while traveling to Gettysburg.

Lincoln with his personal secretaries
John Nicolay (left) and John Hay (right)

How Did the Myth Get Started?

One of the earliest mentions of Lincoln writing the speech on the train appeared in 1882. That year, John Usher, a cabinet member for Lincoln, gave a widely publicized speech. Usher said that the Gettysburg Address was "written in the [train] car . . . from Washington to the battlefield, upon a piece of pasteboard held on his knee."

John Usher

This idea became a common feature of the train myth. In 1885, writer Isaac Arnold claimed Lincoln wrote the speech on the train. The tale was repeated in "The Perfect Tribute," a popular short story written by Mary Shipman Andrews in 1906.

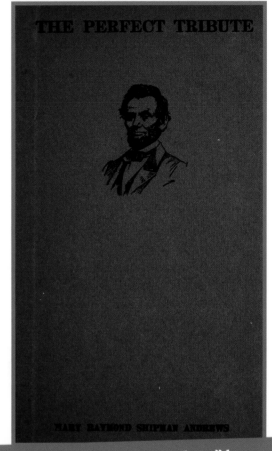

Cover of "The Perfect Tribute" by Mary Shipman Andrews

In Andrews's story, Lincoln hastily wrote the speech on a torn piece of brown wrapping paper on the train. The story found its way into schoolbooks and was later the subject of two movies.

How Did Lincoln Really Write the Address?

On November 17, the day before his departure, Lincoln wrote the first part of the speech in ink on White House **letterhead**. He carried this paper in his coat pocket on the train ride to Gettysburg. Then at David Wills's house on November 18, Lincoln added more to the speech and made changes in pencil.

Lincoln holding his Gettysburg Address as he speaks at the event

The next morning, Lincoln toured the Gettysburg battlefield, where he saw many tombs and graves. He returned to his room at the Wills house and made further changes to the speech. These changes reflected the deep emotions he had felt while touring the battlefield.

Speaking at the ceremony, Lincoln held two sheets of paper. One was written in ink, the other in pencil. These sheets—and last-second changes he made as he spoke—are the Gettysburg Address.

WHAT DID LINCOLN ACTUALLY SAY?

There are five existing copies of the Gettysburg Address in Lincoln's handwriting. Lincoln gave them as gifts to friends. No two copies are exactly the same. Many historians believe Lincoln gave the copy used at the ceremony to his secretary, John Nicolay. Others believe that copy has been lost.

Chapter Three

A Nation Responds

Another myth concerning the Gettysburg Address is that everyone admired the speech. In fact, Lincoln's speech drew both positive and negative reactions.

Edward Everett had finished his speech. At about 2:00 p.m., Lincoln rose from his seat on the guests' platform and walked to the speaker's stand. Newspaper reports described Lincoln as "sweating" and "**listless**." In fact, Lincoln was sick with the early stages of **smallpox**. When he returned to the White House after the event, he had to stay in bed for about three weeks.

Accounts of the events that followed vary widely. Some newspapers reported that Lincoln was greeted with loud cheering. Others said the welcome was friendly or completely silent. Some observers said Lincoln delivered the speech from memory. The *Cincinnati Daily Commercial* reported Lincoln read his address from "a paper."

SPEECH OF THE PRESIDENT.

The PRESIDENT then appeared at the foot of the platform, and, upon being introduced by the Marshal, was vociferously cheered by the vast audience. He spoke as follows:

"Four score and seven years ago our fathers brought forth on this continent a new nation, conceived in liberty and dedicated to the proposition that all men are created equal. [Applause] Now we are engaged in a great civil war, testing whether that nation, or any other nation so conceived and so dedicated, can long endure. We are now on a great battle-field of that war. We are met to dedicate a portion of it as the final resting-place of those who here gave their lives that that nation might live. It is altogether fitting and proper that we should do this. But, in a larger sense, we cannot dedicate, we cannot consecrate, we cannot hallow this ground. The brave men, living and dead, who struggled here have consecrated it far above our poor power to add or to detract. [Applause.] The world will little note nor long remember what we may say here; but it can never forget what they did here. [Applause.]

It is for us, the living, rather to be dedicated here to the unfinished work that they have thus far so nobly carried on. [Applause.] It is rather for us here to be dedicated to the great task remaining before us; that from this honored day we take increased devotion to that cause for which they here gave the last full measure of devotion; that we here highly resolve that these dead shall not have died in vain. [Applause.] That the nation shall, under God, have a new birth of freedom; and that Governments of the people, by the people and for the people, shall not perish from the earth. [Long-continued applause.]

Excerpt of an article from The *Weekly National Intelligencer* shows Lincoln's speech and audience applause.

The President Speaks

As the president spoke, "The crowd was hushed into silence," said Andrew Curtin, the governor of Pennsylvania. "Hats were removed and all stood motionless," wrote Robert Miller, who had attended the dedication. Several reports claimed people cried during the speech. When Lincoln stopped speaking, "scarcely could an untearful eye be seen," wrote an Ohio reporter.

Newspapers that supported Lincoln's presidency claimed the speech was a huge success. *The Springfield Republican* wrote, "His little speech is a perfect gem; deep in feeling . . . tasteful and elegant." The *Chicago Tribune* declared Lincoln's remarks "will live among the annals of man." American politician Charles Sumner called the speech "a monumental act" and that the world "will never cease to remember it."

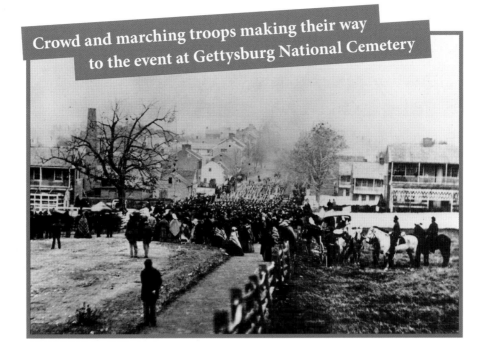

Crowd and marching troops making their way to the event at Gettysburg National Cemetery

Fact!

An estimated crowd of 10,000 to 20,000 people attended the Gettysburg National Cemetery dedication ceremony.

Mixed Reaction

A few papers that opposed Lincoln's presidency criticized the speech. *The Patriot & Union* out of Harrisburg called Lincoln's words "silly remarks . . . that they shall be no more repeated or thought of." The *Chicago Times* wrote that the speech was "silly" and "flat." A reporter from *The Times* of London called the speech "dull and commonplace."

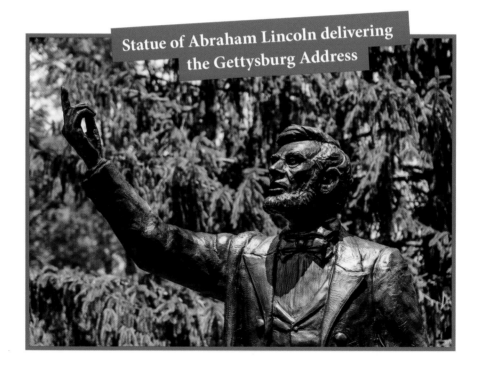

Statue of Abraham Lincoln delivering the Gettysburg Address

What Did Lincoln Think of the Speech?

It was rumored that Lincoln was disappointed in his speech, but that is also a myth. True, he had humbly called his speech "stray thoughts." But Lincoln believed he had accomplished what he set out to do at Gettysburg. He had honored the soldiers who had died at Gettysburg and spoke of a better future for his nation.

THE EVERETT LETTER

The day after the dedication, Lincoln received a letter from Edward Everett. Everett wrote, "I should be glad, if I could flatter myself that I came as near to the central idea of the occasion, in two hours, as you did in two minutes." Lincoln later said that he had "never received a compliment he prized more highly."

Chapter Four

The Legacy of Lincoln's Words

One final mystery surrounds the Gettysburg Address. Where was Lincoln standing when he gave the speech? In July 1869, the Soldiers' National Monument was dedicated at the Gettysburg National Cemetery. The tall stone monument honors the fallen Gettysburg soldiers.

Soldiers' National Monument at Gettysburg National Cemetery

The last four lines of the Gettysburg Address are carved into the base of the monument. For nearly 125 years, it was widely believed the monument stood at the exact site of Lincoln's speech.

As it turns out, it does not. Lincoln actually spoke a short distance from the monument. He spoke from inside Evergreen Cemetery, which is outside the Gettysburg National Cemetery. An iron fence now separates the two.

Evergreen Cemetery, where Lincoln actually spoke, is on the other side of the iron fence.

Words That Matter

In his speech, President Lincoln declared that the struggle for freedom, equality, and national unity must be continued. His powerful words have stood the test of time. His call for a "new birth of freedom" is as important now as it was more than 150 years ago.

The Lincoln Speech Memorial at Gettysburg National Cemetery honors Lincoln's Gettysburg Address.

Mythology of the Gettysburg Address

Fiction President Abraham Lincoln was the main speaker at the dedication of the Gettysburg National Cemetery.

Fact Edward Everett was the main speaker at the dedication.

Fiction Lincoln hastily wrote his speech while on the train traveling to Gettysburg, Pennsylvania.

Fact Lincoln carefully created the Gettysburg Address over a period of several days.

Fiction All Americans immediately admired Lincoln's speech.

Fact While most of Lincoln's supporters praised the speech, some people were disappointed, and some criticized the speech.

Fiction Lincoln was disappointed by his performance and played down the importance of his speech.

Fact Lincoln once referred to the speech as "stray thoughts," but he was not critical of the speech. He had accomplished what he set out to do: honor the soldiers who died at Gettysburg and call for a "new birth of freedom" for his countrymen.

Glossary

cabinet (KAB-uh-nit)—a group of advisors for the head of a government

dedication (ded-i-KAY-shun)—the opening of a place with a special ceremony

inspiration (in-spuh-RAY-shuhn)—a sudden brilliant, creative, or timely idea

letterhead (LET-ur-hed)—stationery with a printed heading stating a person's or organization's name and address

listless (LIST-les)—without energy or enthusiasm

politician (pawl-uh-TISH-uhn)—a person who runs for or is elected to a position in government

smallpox (SMAWL-pahks)—a disease that causes a rash, high fever, and blisters

solemn (SAH-luhm)—very serious

vain (VAYN)—useless or producing no result

Read More

David, Alex. *Examining the Gettysburg Address by Abraham Lincoln*. New York: Enslow Publishing, 2021.

Orr, Tamra. *Abraham Lincoln's Gettysburg Address*. North Mankato, MN: Cherry Lake Publishing, 2020.

Sjonger, Rebecca. *Abraham Lincoln: The Gettysburg Address*. New York: Crabtree Publishing, 2019.

Internet Sites

Battle of Gettysburg
kids.britannica.com/kids/article/Battle-of-Gettysburg/625739

Gettysburg Address
american-historama.org/1860-1865-civil-war-era/gettysburg-address.htm

What Was the Gettysburg Address?
wonderopolis.org/wonder/What-Was-the-Gettysburg-Address

Index